TRUTH

Women In Ministry Business Owners Tell Their Story of Being Leaders in Ministry & Business

i

Dedication

This book is dedicated to all current and future Church Girl CEO's who thought they couldn't make it but have taken their stand to walk in their purpose while on the road to their destiny. They will lead in in their ministries and business with great honor and grace that God has bestowed upon you. You have proven that you will be a leader in ministry and business.

Table of Contents

A Message from our Visionary

Truth is defined as the body of real things, events and facts: ACTUALITY.

Sitting here wondering what to write or how I would contribute to this project has been a challenge. All of the turbulence that is surrounding me acting as a distraction to where I need to be doing. All I could say is God not my will, but your will be done.

When you realize what your purpose is and how it works with your destiny you don't have time to pay attention to the distractions that are coming your way. All you can do is continue on your path that God has predestined for you. Pull yourself up look in that mirror and continue to say 'I Can Do This!' 'I've Been Created for This!' 'Take That Devil, I'm Still Here!' 'My life Matters!'

When reading these words of "TRUTH", I pray you are inspired to move forward and know that you too can make it. You have the endurance and the tenacity to make it to the next level, God is calling you too.

Chapter 1

God's Property LLC

- Cynthia Brown

Jeremiah 29:11 "For I know the plans I have for you, declares the Lord, plans to prosper you and not to harm you, plans to give you hope and a future."

When God has a purpose and plan for you, he takes full control of your life and your future. From the very beginning, before we were created in our mother's womb, God had a divine plan already set in place for our lives. Jeremiah 1:5 declares "Before I shaped you in the womb, I knew all about you..." It is up to us to follow that plan in order to fulfill our divine purpose. In spite of the destiny set before us, there will be opposition along the way to try to derail our progress. It will take perseverance and determination to overcome the twists and turns that come with life.

Advancing through life, I really thought I was making my own decisions, but all along God was in control, navigating my life in the direction that he had for me. At times, I had no idea what was taking place, but God was behind the scenes pushing and advancing me towards my purpose, reminding me that he was in control. For over 30 years, I have been in the commercial real estate business. It's a very tough business, but I have been very successful, and it has been fulfilling, but not without hard work, sacrifice and setbacks.

From a young person growing up in the 60's-70's, a passion was birthed in me to become a successful businesswoman. I have no clue of where this desire came from, being that my Mom and most of the women that I grew up around were housewives. Although I admired them, I was driven by my desire to be an independent and powerful woman in business. I would imagine myself in boardrooms, making important decisions, holding positions of power and influence. I had no idea how I would accomplish this goal since it seemed like the odds were stacked against me. I didn't know anyone to show me the way, I was not from a wealthy family of influence, I was a quiet church girl. I really had not been anywhere or done anything, yet I had great expectations for myself.

By middle school, I had narrowed my decision down to becoming a stockbroker, lawyer, banker, psychologist, or maybe a newscaster. I had little knowledge in these areas of business, but they seemed to be exciting and would help me fulfill my passion of being a successful businesswoman. I remember saving my allowance each week to buy popular magazines such as Vogue, Essence, and Mademoiselle. I studied and scoured every page in those magazines... from the beautiful suits, blouses, dresses, purses, shoes, hairstyles, makeup, perfumes and accessories. I wanted to be prepared when I entered the business world, from top to bottom.

While these were exciting times, they were uncertain times as well because being a powerful businesswoman did not seem to be anyone's dream but mine. I didn't really have a role model until high school, when I was introduced to a successful African-American woman, who had her own business consulting firm. It was an "Ah Ha" moment for me. I began working for her when I was just sixteen years old. I was hired to simply answer her phones, but as time went on, she entrusted me with her filing, typing letters, making phone calls, setting appointments, bookkeeping, attending meetings with her, planning luncheons, holiday parties and even typing a book. She was now my mentor and I followed her lead. She was well educated, professional, drove a beautiful Mercedes and dressed in the latest fashions. God had given me a real-life role model, not someone off the pages of a magazine.

After graduating from high school, I began studying for a degree in Business Law at the local community college because I didn't have the opportunity to go away to college. At the age of eighteen, I married the love of my life, Ronald Brown. We had grown up together in our local church and our families were well connected. For a while I worked at a small bank, but soon became bored and was headed to the big city looking for a big career opportunity. I took a temporary job working for a very well-known real estate developer in Washington, D.C. It was at this moment where things began to take a turn, and I started to see the dream and passion that was placed inside of me began to come to life.

That developer hired me full-time, and I stayed at that job for more than nine years moving swiftly up the corporate ladder. I was one of the youngest members of my firm and was determined to learn everything I could about the world of commercial real estate. It was a tough competitive business, but I began making exceptionally good money and had the opportunity to work on all types of commercial projects, such as office buildings, industrial warehouses, apartment projects, condominiums, and hotels. This was such an exciting time for me to learn about a business that would change the trajectory of my life forever. I was introduced to some of the wealthiest and most-influential people in the city. We were always entertaining Mayor Marion Barry, City council members, bankers, lawyers, architects, engineers and other business partners in our offices as we put together business deals. I fell in love with the real estate business and the entire process of development.

While advancing my career, I also became a mother to two beautiful baby boys, Ronald, Jr. and Carlos. It was an exciting time in my life! Then along came a major real estate crash and recession in the early 90's. My company experienced a major restructuring, we lost a lot of properties that I was managing at the time and I was ultimately laid off. Although I was devastated at the time, it turned out to be a blessing in disguise. Once again, I would see God's hand of mercy guiding me to my destiny. I was given a significant severance pay which gave me the opportunity to stay home for a while and care for my two babies. While I was home, I made good use of my time, by passing the Maryland State Exam to become a licensed Real Estate License and opening a home-based business filling positions with Home Health Care Aides and Nannies.

Just as I was getting tired of working from home, a local real estate developer hired me to help build his family-owned real estate portfolio. I was ready for a new challenge. The company had a significant amount of raw land ready for development and cash to purchase new properties, thus giving me a great opportunity to spread my wings. It was at this point that I decided to go to the next level of my career and began studying for my Real Estate Brokers Exam. I passed and opened my own Real Estate Company in 2002. My love for real estate has grown over the years and has given me the opportunity of a lifetime. With God ordering my steps, I have successfully overseen major real estate projects, from conception to completion. This was another area where I saw the hand of God, because at the time, it was not common for women to be in the real estate development business and especially with skin that looked like mine. I was recognized for being a tough negotiator and was called the "Queen Bee of Real Estate" due to my sweet disposition but ability to close a business deal. There were times I was not treated fairly in business deals, overlooked in news articles and cheated out of commissions, but it did not stop my progress or determination.

Finally, one day I realized that I had fulfilled my dream of becoming a successful businesswoman in the commercial real estate business. I also realized that after developing hundreds of acres of land, selling over $200 million in real estate and building an investment portfolio for others, I had not accomplished much for my family. I began saving every commission and investing in our futures. Through much prayer and direction from God, my husband and I are successful entrepreneurs and real estate investors.

To my surprise, God also had a divine spiritual path for my life. Although my husband and I were active in ministry at our local church, God began to unfold an even greater purpose in our lives. Following the leading of the Holy Spirit, my husband and I accepted the call to Pastor and stepped out on faith, opening our church, Life in Victory Outreach Ministries. Never in my own plans had I wanted to Pastor, but it was in the plan of God, and we submitted to his will. We have now been pastoring a wonderful church for thirteen years. Throughout our journey of establishing and serving in ministry, I've been able to use the wisdom and knowledge that God had given from my career experience to help guide the business side of ministry.

Sure, there are things along the way that I could have done differently but following God's path will never lead you wrong. When God gives you a burning passion, seek him for direction and wisdom on how to execute that desire.

From a spiritual aspect, I know now that allowing myself to become God's property was the greatest accomplishment that I could ever imagined for myself. I was focused on fulfilling my personal desires, while all along, God was unfolding a greater spiritual plan for my life. It's amazing how God orchestrates his will for our lives while still granting us our desires. I encourage you to make your petitions unto God, let him know what dreams and desires you have, but then allow His plan to be manifested in your life.

Co-Pastor Cynthia Brown

Biography

Co-Pastor Cynthia Brown has been married to the love of her life, Bishop Ronald L. Brown, Sr. for 35 years, and together they have three children, one daughter-in-law, one son-in-law and six beautiful grandchildren.

Co-Pastor Brown has assisted her husband in Pastoring Life in Victory Outreach Ministries since the church we established in 2007 and was appointed as Co-Pastor in June 2017. She is the founder of the "Women of War Prayer Ministry" and hosts a weekly "Breakthrough Prayer Call" which is designed to strengthen Intercessors and encourage

Women of God how to effectively and strategically war against the enemy through prayer.

She has earned Certificates in Biblical Studies at Evangel Cathedral Central Bible School and Calvary Bible Institute and is currently furthering her studies in Christian Counseling at West Coast Bible College.

Co-Pastor Brown is an anointed psalmist who began singing in the church as a young child and has found her ultimate purpose in life is serving the people of God and building the Kingdom. She is a humble servant, a Prophetic voice, a true Worshiper and an Intercessor for the body of Christ.

Her motto for victorious living is, a quote by the famous poet Maya Angelou that says *"...When you know better, do better!"* One of her favorite scriptures is, *"...Thanks be to God, which giveth us the victory through our Lord Jesus Christ." I Corinthians 15:57*

Chapter 2

The Promise from Adversity to Assignment

Rosalind "Roz" Jones

There are only twenty-four hours a day. Believe it or not, I was using every moment of the day to work and make everyone else happy including my husband. There were many times that I gave up exercise classes, going to the spa to get a pedicure, getting my hair done, shopping with my girlfriends, going out to the movies with friends, or not visiting my family on special occasions. I always supported my husband's vision of being a Pastor. Heck, I made sure that I paid the church's light bill, paid for the church musician, paid for the church building insurance, and let's not forget I even paid for the expenses when my husband and I traveled. The sacrifices I made never seemed to benefit me. My issues did not stop there as I owned a business. Wouldn't you know it my employees and husband were happy, but I was miserable? I felt like a hamster running on the wheel and going nowhere fast.

As a newlywed our marriage was awesome, I could not wait to get home to see my husband and spend time with him. All was well until we had our first disagreement, he became angry because of the business decision I made without discussing it with him. Wait, I thought, "I'm grown and the last time I looked in the mirror I surely appeared to be an adult. I'd been a decision-maker long before he came along. In the early stage of the marriage, we still operated with a single mind. Hee felt as if I had disrespected him by not including him in my decision-making process. However, that was never my intention.

As much as I hated to admit it, I was consumed with my business, and he was naturally consumed with the church which he pastored. Over the following months, my husband began to complain that I was not spending enough time at home. It was clear that he wasn't happy. But wait, he never felt that he was spending as much time away as I had. I never complained so I felt blind-sided, to say the least.

I began to make the adjustments in time away since I thought that would make him happy. I spent more time at the church and became involved in what interested him. I began to lose myself and became the church wife I thought he wanted. If he asked me to attend a meeting, I was there. If he needed money for a church project or church expenses, I would use money from my business to make sure the church and his needs were met. I made sure that I adjusted my work schedule to be at every church event and to be on the front row of every speaking engagement as was expected of a "First Lady." At least, I thought I was doing things he desired to see in "his church wife." Previously, I dressed in my own style. I thought I could be myself. But then he started complaining of the clothes and behaviors that he thought was becoming of a First Lady. I would hear "your skirt is too high" or "you need a girdle on" and my response was always "you are worried about the wrong stuff." I had no clue about the things he ridiculed me for. I was cute and on mute. No one could teach me how to be the first lady, I had to do on the job training and observe others and imitated until I came into my own style that made him happy. Wearing the long dresses, girdle, big hats, and pantyhose seemed to be the uniform of the First Ladies. It made him happy. I lost my identity; I was miserable and wearing all of those made me sweaty. But this seemed to put our marriage back on track for a few years pretending to be someone I wasn't. I dreamed of the vacations that we never went on. One day I realized that I had not seen my parents since the marriage and often asked him to go home with me but there was always an excuse. He would always tell me he didn't want to go out of town because he didn't have money. However, it was okay to go out of town for a church event using the money from my business. So, if he was happy, I continued to make the sacrifices.

There were special moments we had together early in the marriage but it all seemed to fade away after a few years. We used to pray together and study the word. This turned into me only hearing him pray and talk about the word on Sunday morning. There were times when I was washing dishes, he would squeeze my butt or kiss me on the neck. Let me not forget, those 2 am sex Capades and all-night snuggling. Eventually, it all turned into us sleeping on opposite sides of the bed (at the edge) of the king-size bed and using paper plates to avoid contact.

The bigger the problems the less he talked to me, but he would seek other opinions on our marriage. Then he would always tell me what others had to say about our marriage. This made me FISH GREASE hot. How in the HELL can you ask someone else about the problems in our marriage and not even talk to your wife? This is when I felt as if the enemy was infiltrating and destroying the marriage.

The problems from the marriage began to impact my ability to be successful in the business. I forgot my business why, wasn't so focused, forgot the vision, lost the passion, didn't follow the business plan when a client ended services, or died to replace the lost income. When I didn't keep up with my business responsibilities my team suffered due to lack of leadership. I also had four clients died within a six-month period which was a 6-figure income loss. I felt as though I was in a tug of war between my husband and business. I thought my marriage was more important and if I could get that back on track then the business would follow. Well, that didn't happen. I lost good employees, the business reputation suffered, and I had to go back to work full time for us to survive. I still was in denial that my sacrifices were not enough.

At this point, I was doing what I thought was necessary to balance my marriage and business. I was using money from the business to pay house and church expenses. I knew this was wrong when you are in survival mode your thoughts and actions are truly different. I was living day to day juggling money from one account to another. Always making payment arrangements on past due bills, trying to beat bill collectors and Non-Sufficient Fund charges. This was happening because the church membership dropped from seventy-five to less than five whole people. Yes, that's what I said, and I was trying to save my husband's creditability again. The first time I helped was when my husband was awarded a city recreation center through a federal grant. They sent him a ten thousand dollar draw for repairs on the center before we were married, and he used it for the church expenses. I did not find out about the misuse of the money until he wasn't able to pay it back and there was a probability of him going to jail. So, I had to borrow from my family, friends, and my 401k retirement plan to keep him out of jail. I should have been put in jail for stupidity. I was in love! I surely did not want to see my husband go to jail for unscrupulous matters. How often do I keep helping and sacrificing? I guess I am like Tina Turner clone, "What's Love got to do with it."

As I stated before I lost four clients in a six-month period which was a six-figure loss to the business. It took me two years to get to full business recovery. I didn't market nor advertise for new business. My sole focus was on my marriage and his ministry. This is where I should have asked for help, counseling, or a lifeline. I think at this point I was too proud to ask for help in my marriage. But I knew I had the help needed for the business or we would never survive. Talking to my husband was like talking to a brick wall when it came to my business. Even though he had been a business owner for more than 10 years prior to our marriage. He seldom offered assistance in the business, this was hurtful when I desperately wanted his help. Seeing him help others and not put the same efforts into our marriage or business was like a knife in my heart. I feel like those he stole and the opportunity for us impact the lives of others and be a powerful couple. All of the signs were there however love is blind and we don't really see the negatives of a relationship that shouldn't be.

Rosalind Jones, award-winning professional speaker and three-time Amazon Best-Selling Author, is virtual caregiver coach dedicated to taking the proactive approach to working with caregivers and their loved ones positively impacting their quality of life. She also serves as an advocate, crisis counselor and healthcare intervention. In addition to running Jacksonville's Best Caregivers, Rosalind uses her experience and education to provide training to new caregivers and their family members so they are able to best care for their loved ones.

Chapter 3

From Being Broken To Breakthrough

Noreen N. Henry

How did I move from:

- Thinking I was ugly growing up.
- An emotionally abusive relationship
- Being undervalued
- Trying to change me into someone different, making it that my true self wasn't valuable
- Not loving myself or being true to myself
- Being so broken
- I couldn't cry because of my heart being hard
- Emotional eating and all the bad habits that go along with it
- Rejection, persecution, adultery and abandonment

My journey took a turn when I left the toxic relationship I was in.

But let's start at the beginning. When I was born, words said to me were "what an ugly thing this is." Shocking, right? But they were just words, they were not meant. Or so we thought! Those words got into my spirit and began the course of my life. No one knew how I felt about myself so I never got help with it. I would just have thoughts of being ugly, and I would think, no guy would want me because of it.

Spring forward, I was in my 20s, approx. 25, where I was looking at old photo albums and thinking, I wasn't ugly. I began to wonder where that come from. Why did I think I was ugly when I was growing up? Then, it came back to my memory, the words that were said to me at my birth. I say the words said to me at birth started the course of my life because I thought I was ugly, and being ugly I didn't know to value myself.

I was in a relationship that my former spouse was trying to change me into something I was not. I got criticized, things that were said to me were, "you don't know how to dress," negative comments about my hair, nails, and weight. I was always being put down.

My older son said, mummy, listen to the song "Take Me As I Am" by Mary J. Blige. He understood what was going on and he was just a teenager. I was in the relationship for 20 years before I couldn't do it anymore. The last straw was the adultery.

It was when I left that relationship that I began to be myself again. Also, being out of the relationship showed me that I was in such bondage, and that I had lost myself in the constant fighting (not physically), but encouraging my spouse to do right by my children and myself and the constant fighting to be myself. It shouldn't have been that hard.

I say that "I am back to myself and am even better." When we are in situations for a while, it becomes the norm even though it's not normal. During the relationship, I had developed emotional eating. I was led to write my story about it because it will help others that have struggled to know that they are not alone, it's called "Food Addiction: The Struggle Has Been Real."

I developed emotional eating because I was unhappy, and the thing is, I didn't realize how unhappy I was. When anything was wrong in my relationship, I turned to food, a coping mechanism, and the result of more food increased fat on the body. When I began to gain weight, I was ashamed. I would cut the tags out of my clothes so that no one would see the size. Even though doing that didn't matter because the extra weight on my body could be seen. It was years of eating emotionally before I knew that that was what I was doing. But with knowing that it was emotional eating, it didn't stop the behavior.

It was upon taking the Rhema Bible Study course and one of the required reading was "How to Avoid Tragedy and Live A better Life." Upon reading this book, my life transformed even more. I began to properly work on my inner self. I have always been an avid reader and I bought the book "Healing the Brokenhearted." I bought an emotional healing package from Joyce Meyer Ministries. In doing this, I was on my path to victorious living, even though I didn't know that that was what I was doing at the time ☺.

After a while, my life began to change.

Fast forward to 2015, I got my ordination through Joan Hunter Ministries and I met a couple that we connected and established a relationship. In checking out their ministry, they had inner healing sessions. When I saw that, I thought, that's exactly what I need to help with the hardness of my heart. When I had my first session, the first thing that came up were the words said to me at my birth, and my eyes watered. Wow! When things are not dealt with, they get buried deep inside and affect our lives. I didn't know back then that those words were affecting me.

In 2016, at the beginning of the New Year, I signed up for business classes. This is the time I became passionate about helping others to live victoriously. I had always been the kind of person that wanted the best for everyone, even when I didn't realize how much it was a passion for me until years later.

I began writing books and became a published author. I founded Victorious Living Culture where coaching, etc. helps many to turn their lives around to victory, and that is just the beginning. I'm now a TV talk show host of "Victorious Living With Noreen." What's next? Who knows ☺. I'm just following the leading of my Heavenly Father.

I could have stayed in the relationship I was in and stayed unhappy fighting, (not physically) for my former husband to do what's right by his family. But I made the choice to separate and even though I would think, "did I do the right thing" my life and how I am now shows that I did.

If I had valued myself and had the knowledge I have now, I wouldn't have stayed in the relationship. On the other hand, if I didn't go through all terrible things I did, I wouldn't have such a testimony. It was hard, but I am happy now, joyful, and at peace. Plus, I overcome in my circumstances to victory and have changed my legacy.

You see, even though I was mentally and emotionally abused for years, I've overcome and am an ordained minister. Even though I was told negative things like I'm worthless and made to believe I have no value, I am a multiple #1 international best-selling author.

Even though I was told my smile is too big and I laugh too much, I have a victorious living business. Even though I was in bondage for many years, I am a certified JMT member. Even though I had food addiction for many years, I am an overcomer. Even though I was rejected, persecuted, and abandoned, I have a Victorious Living With Noreen TV Talk Show.

Even though I faced many circumstances that were terrible, I have joy, peace, and happiness everyday no matter what. Plus, I work through my circumstances til I overcome them to victory.

My full story will be available soon.

"There is always hope to live victoriously!"

Noreen N. Henry is a Victorious Living Strategist, who is known for her knowledge, wisdom, and understanding along with instant results. One of her passions is transforming lives from defeat to victory. She is a powerful coach, international speaker, trainer, author, ordained minister, and health educator. She is a multiple #1 international best seller, who authored 10+ books.

Noreen is an ordained minister and is a certified Biblical Counselor. She is a member of the American Association of Christian Counselors, 4 Corners Alliance, John Maxwell Team Member, Toastmasters International, and Promote-Her. Noreen is also certified in: Administrative Assistant, Cake Baking and Decorator, Biblical Counseling, and GSC Leader.

Noreen has been featured on Gratitude Girls, Author in Business, National Black Book Festival, Visions of Greatness Entrepreneur Spotlight, Conversations with Lady Linda, Kingdom Purpose Talk, Courageous Woman Magazine, and other media outlets. She created the "Unleash Your Greatest Potential, Living Your Best Life NOW! Annual Event.

Noreen is passionate about victorious living and cares a great deal about mankind. She is making the world a better place. The song "People Help the People" was dedicated to Noreen by one of her nieces.

Noreen is the mother of three children, and three grandchildren, and resides in New York City. Reach Noreen on www.NoreenNHenry.com.

Chapter 4

From Rock Bottom to Solid Ground

Tiffany Lanae

I remember that cold January night in 2012 like it was yesterday. It was a Friday night, so he typically went to hang out with his friends, or whomever else I wasn't aware of. It could have been one of the women that I would later find out that he slept with. But on this night, the tension had been building. We had an argument before he left and I knew that if "he" came home drunk, the verbal and physical altercation that usually happened at the height of this tension would have been fatal.

I vowed to myself that I would not tolerate another ounce of abuse.

This time, if he tried to hit me, I was going to fight back and use any weapon that I could find. I kept having this horrible feeling in my soul that somebody was going to die that night. I couldn't bare the thought that my son could potentially witness another violent episode between his parents.

We all have heard tragic stories about domestic violence ending with everyone, including the children, dead. I just wanted him to disappear, vanish, never to be seen again. That would have been the answer to my prayers. I certainly wasn't willing to go to jail for him or anyone else. But with each passing moment that night, I became overwhelmed with pressure and fear. Then I clearly heard the Holy Spirit say "GET OUT TONIGHT!"

He only had to say it once, and I listened. No more thinking, "Things will work out, God is going to fix it, I can forgive him and things will get better." I had to seize this moment to escape with my son – it was either now or never. I delayed leaving for ALL of the wrong reasons, like that time just three weeks prior where he tightly squeezed my neck......The thought of that moment caused knots in my stomach and tears to stream down my cheeks.

I packed our bags like the house was on fire. I had called the police and told them I needed an escort due to the history of domestic violence.

The officer arranged the hotel stay and a cab ride from my condo to the hotel. The length of time I had to wait for the cab to arrive was the most grueling time of my life! I was so terrified he would come home earlier than expected, see the bags packed and immediately attack me. I remember standing and shaking the entire time while we waited for our transportation consumed with anxiety and terror. I prayed like never before, constantly pleading the blood Jesus and thank God, my prayers overrode my fear.

About ninety minutes later, the cab arrived. To my utter relief, I walked out of the condo with my son, a few bags of clothes, and never looked back. As I rode in the cab on the way to the hotel, a sense of relief come over me. I exhaled deeply, as the remnants of living in fear for almost five years left my body. It felt so good to be free, finally!

However, the price of my new-found freedom would cost me everything, except my son and a few articles of clothing. Starting our lives over in a shelter on food stamps and welfare was the most humbling experience of my life. I had to deal with homelessness while fighting my abuser in court for a list of issues, starting with obtaining a protective order. Then he had the audacity to file for custody, and I counter-filed for custody and divorce. I spent twenty-two whole days in court in 2012. I applied for jobs but no one hired me. Emaciated from stress, shame and disappointment, I still had another battle to fight – securing education and resources for my son who could barely talk at the age of 4.

We pushed through every obstacle. By the end of 2012, my divorce was finalized, we moved out of the shelter and into transitional housing. My son was placed in an amazing charter school, I bought a new car, and I started attending church services again. We ended the year on a high note.

In 2013, I rejoined the praise team that I served prior to leaving my abusive marriage. Worship carried me through a living nightmare - it literally saved my life. Aside from being a mom, nothing gave me greater joy than to worship God. A year later, I began to evangelize in the DC area, working with The Widow's Pantry to minister to the homeless in Franklin Square Park, two blocks from the White House. I loved serving all of God's people. In 2016, I felt God leading me to begin the journey of becoming a recording artist. I teamed up my friend and ministry partner, Michael Verner, to begin production. After selecting two songs to record, and preparing to go into the studio, Mike passed away suddenly from a massive heart attack during a Sunday afternoon service.

Utterly devastated, I grieved for a few months. I was in complete shock. We planned to release the music and minister to the world. Mike was my biggest cheerleader, and I just couldn't understand why he left us so suddenly. I knew I had to finish the music and release it in his honor. This wouldn't happen without a series of additional setbacks though.

The producer we contracted disappeared after I paid him $3,000 to produce two songs. I tried contacting him for several months. He finally answered, but disappeared again. I asked a few people to reach out to him on my behalf, but no response. I was livid, but after wise counsel, and hearing from God, I decided to move forward without filing a lawsuit. But I had to move forward in faith, because I had no money. I was evangelizing and ministering all over the DC, Maryland, and Virginia area, but barely had enough money to eat, let alone pay my rent.

I had been fired from my administrative job after nearly two years of enduring a hostile work environment, reminiscent of my abusive marriage. After that abrupt termination, I couldn't find work and became so far behind in my rent that my landlord had no other choice but to start eviction proceedings. Worried that I would become homeless again, I had to put my faith in action. I prayed fervently and applied for as many jobs as possible. In the nick of time, God blessed me with employment so that I could pay my rent without getting evicted. My landlord also forgave a debt of over $15,000 in back rent!

So with new employment, a thriving ministry as a psalmist, as well as founding a gospel outreach group called The Village, my life was beginning to align with God's perfect will. But I still hadn't released any music. I found a new producer, recorded the song, but hated how my vocals sounded. After working with my vocal coach, Michelle Beckle for about a year, I started to feel this overwhelming burden to release the song. So I called my producer, and he arranged a studio session. I was exhausted after a long week of work but I had to do this. That Friday night, we recorded the song with just my voice, the piano, and the Holy Spirit. Within three weeks, and just days after Mike's birthday, I released the song and within a month, my calendar was filled with tour dates across the country. "We Want More" received radio airplay in over fifty countries, and my group, The Village, became incorporated as a 501 (c)3 non-profit organization before the year ended.

An abundance of grace and mercy carried me through this journey from homelessness to becoming a Church Girl CEO. Though plagued with several setbacks and obstacles, I refused to be defeated. I preached to myself in the mirror, journaled consistently for a whole year to release the bitterness, shame and unforgiveness that was blocking my future. Four keys to my victory were forgiveness, faith, obedience and perseverance. I encourage anyone with a promise from God to pray, follow His instructions, and watch him take you from rock bottom to solid ground.

** "We Want More" and other music from Tiffany Lanae is available on all digital outlets. For more information, visit www.tiffanylanae.org and subscribe to the mailing list to receive exclusive updates.

Born on the south side of Chicago, Tiffany L. Durden is the 5th of 9 children who all possess musical gifts. As the daughter of a pastor, Tiffany enjoyed singing at her home church, House of Prayer Temple Church of God in Christ, and even started an A' cappella gospel group at her high school, Morgan Park H.S., called AFRICAA Ensemble.

Tiffany relocated to Washington, DC to attend Howard University, where she continued her passion for singing through many choirs and local gospel groups, including the Howard University Community Choir and the BET Urban Nation HIP HOP Choir. She is an ordained Evangelist and serves as Worship Leader for New Wineskins Covenant Assembly in Annandale, VA. She also ministers at various churches and events across the country, sharing the gift of song through prophetic worship. In August 2019, Tiffany released her highly anticipated debut single "We Want More", which is currently ranked at the top of independent gospel charts and in rotation on radio stations across the globe. She recently garnered a 2020 GCMA nomination for Female Artist/Vocalist of the Year. Additionally, Tiffany has had the honor of serving as Musical Director the multi-award winning stageplay, TORN for the past three years.

In June 2017, she founded The Village, a faith-based organization focused on evangelism through the arts. It serves as a bridge between the unchurched and the local church to reach souls for the Kingdom of God through various music initiatives. In October 2019, The Village established itself as a 501-c3 non-profit organization, with plans to expand into new areas of arts outreach. In January 2020, The Village received a Community Service Award from The Widow's Pantry Inc. for their faithful ministry to the Washington, DC's homeless population.

Tiffany resides in Washington, DC and is the proud mother of a son in middle school

Chapter 5

I Want It All

Amy Philpott

"Mom, you don't spend enough time with me."

Those words, of my then 6 year old son, stung worse than any other type of hurt imaginable...***because he was right.***

But, how did we get here?

In 2013, my husband Benji and I discussed finding another avenue of income that would bring in extra money, not take up much family time - preferably something we could do together, and would have a positive impact in our community. We found that with a direct sales company.

As Wayside Gems, we hit the ground excited and running. This opportunity was doing just as we had hoped it would. It allowed us so much creative freedom and was an amazing opportunity to meet and help so many people. Our team was steadily growing and new clients seemed to be finding us every week. It was great. While I was the face of our growing business, our family helped in many ways. Our parents were great with keeping children during events and helped out at events.

Life started changing for us. Our family was growing, and in 2014, our daughter, Clara, was born. In 2016, Benji founded

Wayside Tech to provide IT Services geared towards small and medium sized businesses. Then in 2017, our son Sam was born. During all of these life-changing events, Wayside Gems continued to thrive.

Along with sales increasing, my unhappiness was too. Just like most families, we fell into this daily pattern of work/school, homework, dinner, bath, bed – repeat! Mamas – do you ever feel like this? Stuck in an unhealthy pattern like a broken merry-go-round? I had no idea what to do about it. **I wanted it all.** I wanted to be home with my kids and run this amazing business. I didn't even know where to begin so I just did nothing.

Most families have two parents working with kids raised in daycare. These days it is the norm, but it is not what we had envisioned for our family.

What were we supposed to do? I knew what I wanted to do, and that was to hand in my resignation to my corporate career, but with a family of 5, it didn't seem like the income from my jewelry business was consistent enough to replace my income and the ever rising cost of insurance. Benji and I tried to figure things out, but we kept coming up short or had too many questions unanswered. While this was going on, we were in the middle of finding a new church, two of my top producers were leaving the business (each for major health issues), and then I struggled with feeling like I was being selfish. If I came home permanently and it didn't work out, I felt like it would all be on me. The odds truly seemed stacked against us to find a viable solution.

Hearing our struggles one evening, Frank came into the room and said, "Mama, Daddy, let's just pray about it. God will answer you." Out of the mouth of babes comes a divine inspiration.

We prayed, God answered.

Isaiah 40:31(NIV) states *"Those who wait for the Lord will gain new strength."* We didn't have to do it alone! It is amazing how once we turned it over to God, how simple the process became - not easy, but simple. With every roadblock we faced, I wondered if it was just a sign from God saying this is NOT the path I have for you. With every dead end, my frustration grew. It took patience and time (8 long months) to not only get our plan in place, but to work smarter to grow our businesses faster than we ever thought possible, meet the right people at the right time, and feed our spirit as well. We even found a new church home! We could see God answering our prayers. The Holy Spirit truly knew how to order our steps.

In 2018, everything was falling into place and our hurdles had all been jumped. All but one. While I had surrendered everything else over to God, I had never let go of that guilt of feeling selfish. Rarely have I ever put my wants/needs ahead of others and even more so now that we had a big family. I just couldn't force myself to turn in my notice. My job was my security blanket, but my heart knew I should be at home.

While on vacation, we visited a church. The preacher's message on Bethesda was life changing. In the Gospel of John, Jesus asked this lame man at the pool if he wanted to be healed. Instead of answering Jesus, he gave Him an excuse. _Holy ham sandwiches_ - **THIS WAS ME!!!** God was asking me what the desire of my heart was and all I could do was give Him excuses. He had proved himself over and over. Then the preacher asked one question, "What has you stuck? Just pick up your mat and walk." So I did. Benji and I agreed it was time. Though honestly, I think Benji had been ready, but knew I had to have peace. The next time I saw my boss, I put in my notice.

So now what? The excitement of raising my kids and running a business with my family was amazing. But it didn't mean the challenges stopped.

Life isn't always easy when you transition from the Executive Suite filled with contracts and compliance to being the Executive Sweeper of goldfish and cheerios. There were days in the first few months that I questioned EVERYTHING! How would I do this? How do I not let my work take priority over my family again? Finding that balance took trial and error and whole lot more prayer. What helped was finding like-minded Christian women who were in similar life situations as me. I found support with The Savedpreneur Society and Church Girl CEO. These fabulous groups helped me realize that it wasn't enough to just pray for my business. God needed to be more involved. He needed to be my _business partner_.

Through this, our family business changed to our family ministry. He showed me that our children were learning things that most children aren't even exposed to until they are in school. Beyond colors and patterns, they were learning how to engage with people they don't know and how to pray with others. As new inventory came in, Facebook live shows, or events they attended, they each brought something to the table. They learned that they added value to this business. Most importantly, they knew they mattered!

Above all, I want to inspire moms that living this dream is possible. It is possible to run a business from home and raise your children. The truth bomb that my son delivered hurt, but looking back, I can see how the Holy Spirit was speaking through him to be the catalyst to put God's plan in place. *It is possible to have it all and have two entrepreneurial parents.* So Mamas...what has you stuck? It's time to trust God, pick up your mat and walk into what He has called you to do.

Wife, mom, teacher, volunteer, prayer warrior, The Queen of Bling, all these titles could be used to describe Amy Philpott, but the things that people see through all of these hats and titles are her spirit of servanthood and love of her family. Amy's goal is to show women how they can stay home, raise their kids and run a successful home business with their family. It is possible to have it all, she is living proof.

Amy resides in Shelbyville, TN with her husband, Benji and their 3 children, Frank, Clara, and Sam. They are members of Fair Haven Baptist Church where they serve in several areas of ministry. Amy also volunteers at her children's school with math fluency as well as running club. She is also a member of the Savedpreneur Society, Church Girl CEO, and a 20-year member of the Order of the Eastern Star.

Together they work their family business. This family dynamic approach has earned them much recognition and multiple advancements. Amy also retired from her longtime corporate career at the age of 40 to raise her children and focus more on Wayside Gems. For fun, the family likes to help out on their multi-generational century farm, camping, dancing, and anything with Cub Scouts.

Born and raised in the suburbs of Chicago, Amy attended James B. Conant High School. She later earned her degree in Math and Science from Grand Valley State University in Allendale, Michigan.

Amy Philpott
On the web: **waysidegems.com**
Facebook: **facebook.com/waysidegems**
Instagram: **wayside_gems**
Email: thewaysidegems@gmail.com

Chapter 6

Killing My Comeback

Sonya Floyd

Gazing out of the sunroom window while sipping my morning coffee, I could not stop the tears from falling onto the crumpled pages listing charges of three felony counts, roughly $30,000 in fines, legal expenses, and court fees. But it didn't end there. There was abuse, alcoholism, a failing business, a debilitating knee injury, and greatly diminished financial security. Broke, rejected, emotionally bankrupt, humiliated, and alone.

How I wished this was someone else's story, but you see, this was my living hell. I had absolutely no idea how I got here. Where had it all gone wrong?

My life had been turned upside down and inside out all because of one bad decision: being unequally yoked. I was on the verge of losing everything that I had worked so hard for -- my job, my home, my family -- all over someone who did not care about me.

I will never forget that Saturday afternoon, July 28, 2018, although the taunting began by my adversary on that Friday afternoon. It continued through Saturday with excessive drinking, followed by the 2 a.m. ranting and pacing the floor.

The blatant disrespect and continued mental and emotional abuse led to an explosive altercation.

I had finally reached my breaking point, and I just could not take it anymore. I just wanted it to stop. I wanted the pain to go away. Honestly, it was okay if he didn't love me anymore; I just wanted him to GO!! I was living in my very own Lifetime movie except I couldn't change the channel or turn off the TV.

I had no idea what I was going to do or what life was going to look like going forward. I had never faced a situation like this before. I had always walked the straight and narrow, tried to do the right thing. Truth be told I was in this place because I was so busy running away from God's plan for my life that His voice had become lost amongst all of the chaos in my life.

Little did I know that my legal issues were just the start of an epic avalanche. The day I decided to take back control of my life, I had a terrible accident where I slipped, fell and hit the ground hard. The accident left me with torn ligaments in my left knee and unable to walk for the next 8 weeks. Now my physical state of being torn and in distress matched my mental state. So instead of him leaving, I now had a self-imposed eviction. I ended up having an extended stay with my parents and used that time to sort things out. I recall one of my dearest friends said to me "God wants you to be still; it was not meant for you to go home yet."

I began to think long hard about what my friend had shared with me, and I soon realized YES, God was trying to get my attention, and He wanted me to center myself and listen to His voice for how I needed to move forward. I needed to quiet the noise in my life, those things that were not in my best interest, and begin listening for God's voice.

Now in the middle of the snowball that formed in my life, months later I was *gifted* with unemployment, as my job was being both outsourced and relocated. So here I was in a loveless, lifeless marriage, that was an emotionally and mentally abusive relationship. I was struggling to regain my mobility and now I was jobless. BUT GOD! I knew in my heart that if He had allowed this, it must have been for a reason, and He must have a plan for me.

I can recall asking the Lord why did this happen and what was I supposed to learn from this? I knew in my heart that there had to be a reason, but I needed His help to navigate through this turmoil. I used journaling as a tool to deepen my relationship with the Lord and to draw strength from. I journaled both day and night. When I could not find the words to express what I was feeling, I journaled, focusing on my pain, the scriptures, and prayers. Journaling became my therapy: I found the freedom that I needed through journaling.

I knew coming out of this valley, my life would never be the same. Before all of this, I went to work every day, I did church ministry but what did God desire that I do? With writing down my inner most thoughts, it cleared my mind, which allowed me to hear clearly from God and receive instructions on my next steps. It was through journaling that God revealed my purpose. One day in a still, soft voice the Lord, revealed to me my mandate, which was to lead other women on a "tour" from trauma to triumph. I was to be their Tour Guide and help them through their trauma.

Finally, my Lifetime movie was coming to an end and on a high note. Granted a second chance, I knew my life would be different going forward. I had learned to make lemonade out of the lemons in my life. I'm trusting God with my whole heart and holding fast to His word in every area of my life. I'm gainfully employed again, and my adversary and I are working through our issues. My knee has healed, and not only am I physically able to walk again, but I'm also now walking towards my divine appointment. I have a community of women that I serve and support.

To my dear sisters: It's time to stop running and playing small. Please know that YOU MATTER and your feelings are valid. I cannot express how important it is that you regain control of your life, restore, rebuild, rebrand, and *kill* your comeback.

My Bible became my light in the darkness. During that trying time, here are a few scriptures that helped me navigate through the troubled waters in my life. All are taken from the New King James Version (NKJV) unless noted otherwise:

God promises never to leave us nor forsake us. Hebrews 13:5:

And by His stripes, THANK God I am healed. Isaiah 53:5

---

*God says He will not only rescue and
protect us, but He will answer us when we
call. Psalms 91:14-15 (NLT)*

I was down and there were those that counted me out, but now
I'm back with a vengeance and unstoppable!

Whether you are looking to a throw an over the top lavished event or host your signature event Sonya can put it all together for you. Sonya's been planning social and business events for over 10 years. Sonya is the founder and creative director of Moments That Matter a boutique event planning firm that specializes in creating both live and virtual signature events for women owned service-based businesses. A true entrepreneur at heart and has a love for her ministry. Because you matter is Sonya's mantra, she has a passion for helping women reach their goals and dreams. She is current pursuing her certification in Life Coaching, with emphasis in Goal Setting for Success. Sonya has started a blog Inspire Uplift Ignite inspired by her journey from trauma to triumph and an online community of the same name where women can find encouragement and support.

Follow my blog at www.inspireupliftignite.com. You can email me at Inspireme@InspireUpliftIgnite.com. And if you or someone you know is in a transitional phase of their life and needs the support and accountability of a phenomenal community of women, I invite you to join my Facebook group "Inspire Uplift Ignite" and learn how I killed my comeback and how you can too.

Chapter 7

I Made It

Syreeta Duncan-Bailey

In October 2010, I became a wife to a then minister and two months later, I was a pastor's wife, as you can see that happened quickly. But let me go back a little before I met my husband. I had been divorced from my two children's father for about two years. During that time, I spent a lot of time reconnecting with God and talking to him about what I would like in a future man. I say man because honestly I was not looking to be in a relationship nor ever be married again. Then I met my husband at church September 26, 2010, he was so captivating, and after a few conversations we were inseparable and in strong unexplainable liking of each other, a week later we stood alone just him and I at the courthouse and said I do, with no rings, no witness, just us and our feelings. Like so many others, I know you may be asking yourself WAIT! A week, yep a week. Now let me be clear on this because I have been asked or people have even said, did you marry him because he is a preacher, the answer is NO! I had request to God that he send me a loving man, one that would love me and my kids and show me love like God, a strong man, a funny man, a sensitive man and one after God's own heart and love, I NEVER asked him for a preacher, I wasn't even that much into the church how I was raised, yes I had backslide, we all have. I was a scorned woman, living life having fun, and being a mother, but. Neither one of us could explain why we chose to get married or what led us to the altar; all I can say is just JESUS.

Therefore, now that you have the tea at the beginning. I know you asking yourself, who exactly am I. I am Syreeta Duncan-Bailey, from the capital city of Montgomery, Alabama, I own three professional basketball teams, I am an author and public speaker, I run a non-profit organization River Region Generals Inc., I have a security and entertainment business, and I am a small business and relationship life coach. I am the proud mother of two teenagers Destiny and Xavier, and a forever loving, #MCM (man crush Monday), wife to an amazing hard working man of God, Rev. Antonio M Bailey.

I have always worked in the church even as a young girl my father was a chair deacon and Sunday school superintendent, my mother was over the youth department and my aunt was the church secretary, so I took to her role and became the Sunday school secretary. So in 2010 when God sent my husband to his first church, that was small in number with little to no activities, I was eager to jump head first into helping develop youth activities, church activities, leading prayer intercessory groups and even leading and heading their first women's ministry. I have never been the one to not take on a task, so helping my husband by using my talents, came natural to me. It was being a first lady that I had some struggles with. At times I could be last to speak unless out of anger and I was very hot headed and quick with the tongue, so that first church I learned so much about who I was and what I could do and be and sustain as a leader. I was taught quickly that being a first lady that people always pre judge you and I was a person that had no problem letting you know exactly how I felt. So many people had so many suggestions on what I should say and how I should act as a first lady, I had to learn to listen to God and be my own version of a first lady. After about a 3-4 years service God halted us, it was time for the vision God had given him to be manifested. We left a season and stayed still until God sent us on a new mission this time not as a pastor but an intern pastor at not one but two churches. We learn to balance both of them and still be active with our then young children.

During the course of the next 3-4 years, we went out and did the work of the Lord. Each season and time meeting and loving and praying with many different people, God showed us more and more of ourselves as a couple, as a team, as parents, and as servants to him. It is not easy when God tells you to move because you gain so many relationships and do not want to leave; it is so easy sometimes to become attached to like-minded spirits. During this stint however, I became a business owner and gave birth my basketball franchise. However, here is where God showed me my purpose. I was working at a small private school where by grace I had become a teacher, I played high school and college volleyball so I had the gift of being able to not only help youth in sports but to be able to be on level to communicate and understand them. At that school God showed me many basketball players both good and not so good but he showed me their passion and that is when I moved on my purpose. Needless to my vision was now clear. In December 2017 I decided to become the second African American woman to own her own semi-professional basketball team. Was I excited YES, did I know exactly what I was doing NO, was I terrified yes. My husband had just started on another mission and I was a first lady again and this time around I had mature so much and was so aware of how church people can be, that I said little and smiled often, I was going to be still and not do anything BUT God pushed me introduce women ministry, that was my calling as well, helping women. My time now split from our growing children's sport activities, work, and a new business. This is when my marriage became tested we were now in year 8 of our marriage and even though God was blessing us; our home foundation in our personal life was not strong. We had separated; the church did not even know at the time that arguments to church became fake smiles during church. I was so confused on how this business could be going so well and not be winning in marriage. We manage to live under one roof until now (stay tune for that book).

Women in ministry, that are leaders and business owners we wear so many hats. What I want women to understand is that we still need God. It is so important to me that we share our story of success and how it affects us personally. We have to stay in prayer, keep God first, listen to God and let him show you how to balance it all. This book has come at a great time during COVID-19 were God has made the nation stop. He is making us have no other choice but to call on the name of the Lord. He has taken away the distractions that keep and have kept us away from him; he has silence the noise that makes it hard to hear from him. He has made us make time for him. My prayer is that you see and hear God in your business and use your business to somehow minister to others, God wants us to be a blessing and bless others. If my story on marriage intrigued then be on the lookout for our upcoming new book together "Struggling to Keep the Vows".

Follow me on my Facebook social media Syreeta Duncan Bailey and on my web site

www.syreetaduncanbaile.wixsite.com/website

Syreeta Duncan Bailey is the second African American female to own a professional basketball organization located in the capital city of Montgomery Alabama. Mrs. Bailey has been recognized by many organizations for her leadership both in community and as a female entrepreneur. Currently, It is her goal to use her non profit organization professional basketball to help the youth and her community. She believes it's more than the sport of basketball, but basketball that helps build character, leadership, discipline, determination, and teamwork.

Mrs. Bailey is also the author of, "Life of An Entrepreneur", with two more additional books set to release in 2020, syreeta and her husband have a collaboration book "Struggling To Keep The Vows, and then Mrs. Bailey is releasing, "7 Ways to Keep the Fire in Your Marriage: from your Queens prospective ". Syreeta is a small business, life and relationship coach, and a motivational speaker. She is also the COO of Bailey Enterprise Inc.

Syreeta is a firm believer and a living testimony, that with God nothing is impossible but all things are possible.

https://syreetaduncanbaile.wixsite.com/website/book-online

(334) 787-9251

Chapter 8

Picture I'm Perfect

Tracy Shorter

As I prepared to get ready for the 2008 New Year's Eve service, there was one resolution I had to make. This marriage and family could not remain on its current course because living this lie was too hard. As I looked at our family picture on the mantle, it looked like the perfect recipe for happiness. Girl married her high school sweetheart and built her business with two beautiful kids and a dog.... so, what could possibly be wrong? It was at that moment that I realized I was still CLUELESS about my purpose and role as a wife.

I met my husband my sophomore year of high school and before dating, we were great friends. In high school, I worked hard to be in the room but not seen; my self-esteem was not the greatest because growing up I was always the tallest person in the room, even though I felt like the smallest. Many of the guys growing up with me had not grown into their height yet either, so the interest in dating the tallest girl in class was not popular. So, I focused on my studies and responsibilities with my siblings. It was my responsibility to make sure we all got all from school, started our homework and start dinner. My friends instead were involved in after school club and sports and having so much fun. For me it was like watching a basketball game from the sidelines, my inner person wanted to be on the court, except I kept fumbling the ball due to my lack of confidence. My parents met in high school as well, however, they divorced when I was three or so. When my husband and I married, we were a few months from the birth of our first child. While balancing the new roles as newlyweds, we had to figure out parenthood. The birth of that little girl, we affectionately named Jasmine, really inspired me. I wanted to do everything I could to be the best wife and mom, but still dealing with low self-esteem, I did not feel equipped. I did not have a day-to-day experience to fall back on, as my dad was absent from the home.

The primary advice given to a new bride at her bridal shower is to: "Keep God at the CENTER of your marriage. Be a family that prays together because it helps you stay together," and let us not forget, "Don't have everybody in the business of your marriage." I should have paid closer attention; instead, I took this advice with a grain of salt. My father-in law was a Baptist Pastor, so we both attended church regularly, but still had not made that connection to placing God as the center of our lives.

As my husband and I were going through the motions of life and marriage, our second child was born. Our daily activities began to just be conversations to keep the children on routine, healthy and happy. Life was happening, but we never really talked about the internal problems or allowed the outside world to see our real picture.

As I thought about our relationship and what was going well, we were doing great when it came to the kids, but we lacked supporting each other emotionally. We served as leaders within the church, always supportive to our families and friends, working in our neighborhood association, children's sporting events, and various non-profits. However, we had become *those* people... doing marriage for the love of the kids.

When you are just living for the kids, it's easy to avoid what is really going on between you and your spouse or partner. The kids become an excuse to not talk about the hard things like unrealized dreams, intimacy, communication and of course, finances. At some point if we do our jobs correctly, the children leave the nest. It was those thoughts that had me wondering would we have enough love between us left to make it with just the two of us and be happy? Was growing old together a distant dream? I did not want to gamble on the fact we would still be together once our kids were grown. I desperately still wanted us to work. I talked to my husband about how I was feeling, and I was glad he was open enough to say he had been feeling the same way. After 14 years of marriage, it was then that we decided to try some marriage counseling.

In counseling, we discussed many issues, but the one that rose to the top was the lack of communication. After all these years, one counseling session still stands out to me. We were about halfway into the program and our counselor asked us how the week was going. We immediately laid out this list of blames about lack of cooked meals, unfolded laundry, never hearing the words "thank you or please." They may sound like simple things, but over time, these simple things had created a wide divide. This led to us receiving a communication assignment. The counselor gave us a yellow card to use for the next week called the Communication Card. What we realized at our next session is that we both had horrible listening skills and the way we expressed ourselves to each other was offensive. We had a communication problem, and it boiled down to missing one key element: respect.

As we ended our sessions a few weeks later, all our issues had not disappeared, but a renewed commitment emerged. Change is not always easy, and the process was going to require daily work, with communication as the key.

Some other things we agreed to as part of our rebuilding process were as follows:

1. As a couple we had to make time for each other, above children, family, business, and ministry duties.
2. As individuals, we had issues that shaped us as a couple, so we committed to work on those individually and provide the supported need to help each overcome.
3. As a couple and individually we would seek God for our purpose and support each other in those efforts.

My favorite scripture speaks to number three and is found in Jeremiah 29:11: " For I know the plan I have for you declares the Lord, plans to prosper and not harm, plans for hope and a future". This scripture helped me to see that God's plan for me was one with benefits and a future; I just had to seek His direction for it. Placing God at the center of my life now made sense. Through my personal prayer time and time with God, I understood to be the best wife and mom, I had to first be the best ME. This meant spending time getting to know myself, which included more solo activities and journaling.

A word that has helped me transform even further was BELIEVE. It's simple, but powerful and my self-esteem grew from this word. I have learned to just be myself, that person was capable and more than enough for every role God would position. I understood the importance of having a written vision for our family as it states in Habakkuk 2:2. "Write the vision, make it plain". But most importantly, I learned to take time as a couple and individually and enjoy life, for it is a vital part of the journey. Our lives should not just consist of working all the time, sometimes we just need to stop and enjoy the beauty we have in our family, friends, and the world around us.

I know we were not alone in the struggles we had as a couple, and it is often so silent in families around the world. But if you are reading this and you can relate to any part of this story, I want to encourage you to speak your TRUTH today. Ask God to help you speak to your spouse or partner about getting help with your relationship. Ask God to speak to your heart about what needs to be repaired within yourself. Unresolved issues into any partnership only creates problems that do not go away. When I now think of the future, it with the great excitement that we will be that couple that will grow old together. "Blessed are the ties that bind", instead of our story ending is it just beginning

Whenever you interact with Tracy Shorter one thing for sure is going to happen, you will leave encouraged, supported and have a new cheerleader in this journey we call LIFE! With a strong servant heart and over 12 years of strategic planning experience, she has been helping women fulfill their vision and create memories thru weddings, special events and her non-profit work under Tracy Shorter Enterprises. Tracy is married to her high school sweetheart, Rolando and they have two children, Jasmine and Christian. As an active member in her church, Revelation Knowledge Bible Church she serves as the Financial Director, Deaconess on the Special Event Committee.

Then in 2016, the Lord spoke the word BELIEVE to Tracy and unbeknownst to her she would need it more than ever in 2018 as life did a shift an a unexpected health forecast came without warning. After months of prayer the message to that one simple word BELIEVE was not just clear to Tracy, but that she was to spread that message to those around her. A new purpose unfold, not just to create the beauty of the event, but to help women uncover their purpose and develop a plan to walk and live it every day!

Tracy's story is powerful and could speak to the lives of many women. If you are going in circles trying to find your fit or doing it all for everyone but yourself; then Tracy is the cheerleader you need to help you GET IN THE GAME!

Chapter 9

Rise Above The Setbacks

Selina R. Wells

Twenty years ago, I quit my financially secure job to start my own business as a Credit Restoration Expert. I was so excited. In my first year of business I made six-figures and for two years thereafter, I was living the good life. Then one year later, without warning or a safety net, I got sick and my business went bankrupt.

All I could hear was my father's voice, "Why did you quit that good job?" Then, at that same moment, I heard my inner voice, "you're a failure, and you should have kept your job." These seeds of doubt caused me such internal turmoil, I was constantly waging a mental battle of self-doubt and guilt. It was wearing me out, but I told myself I had to stay strong because I was a single mother and needed to survive this financial crisis for my son.

I consider myself to be a person of strong faith, but this setback caused me a lot of anxiety. I was nervous about my future and how I would recover. It's not so easy to go from being successfully independent to now partnering with someone else, even if it's someone you're dating. I was struggling to accept that I was in a quandary and as I stepped out into the unknown, then the roller coaster ride began.

It's something when you find yourself in a valley. I tried to rely on my faith to get me through this rough patch, but I found myself doubting, feeling insecure and a sense of failure. I would believe the word of God and then not believe; I would have hope and then no hope. In order to survive, I ended up marrying someone that I thought was right for me because he was calm, financially secure and would do anything for me. Although he stabilized my life, I was unhappy and not able to truly be myself in the relationship. I compromised who I was to make the relationship last.

So, after five years of being on an emotional rollercoaster within myself, I made a conscious decision that it was time to make some changes. I ended my relationship with him and transitioned from his church of choice which was a metaphysical church -- a Christian based church that combines religion, science and philosophy. However, I left there spiritually unfulfilled.

As I moved on with my life, I found a new church home that showed me God's love in action. What I mean by this is the people there showed me so much attention, gave me heartfelt conversations and you could really feel the genuineness in their concern for my soul. It was overwhelming at first because I realized up until that point, I never knew God intimately, where I truly allowed myself to be in touch with how much God loves us and His love is infinite. Once I started to look at myself through the same lens that God uses, I saw that I was indeed *fearfully and wonderfully made.*

God wants us to live an abundant life, but in order to walk into that promise, I had work to do. I had to rewire my thinking by focusing on having the right mindset and not looking at vulnerability as a negative but an asset, where it's okay to have moments of sadness and weakness. My feelings of inadequacy were valid, but they did not define me. I had to get my heart and mind delivered from seeing myself as a failure. Then, I was able to accept God's grace and love in my life regardless of what my reality looked like.

I started reading books that helped to shift my mind to think positive and to speak what I wanted to see in my life. I had to train my subconscious mind which is a part of the reticular activating system. We all have done things without thinking about it consciously and subconsciously. Our mind knows by repetition what it's been taught. Whenever my mind started to go back into feelings of inadequacies and thinking things like, "your business will never survive" or "you will never make six figures again" my reticular activation system would kick in and not allow me to think that way. Now, my mind would think on things that are good, lovely and of good report, (Philippians 4:8). My reticular activating system tells me to see myself as confident, secure, loving, genuine, consistent, and in control of my emotions.

This new way of thinking helped me to clean up my life of the many bad decisions I've made while I was on this emotional roller coaster ride. During those years, I lived a thousand lives. I went through a divorce, re-married, divorced again, moved far away from my family, moved back to an urban city from my previous life, started drinking, smoking and the list could go on. I will save all the juicy details for my next book "Christian Style," where I bare my soul on how being emotionally bankrupt can lead you to some destructive decision but with God's grace, you will come out on top, on the other side.

These setbacks could not stop me from giving up on my dreams. All I could think about was rebuilding and restructuring my business. I was an entrepreneur at heart but defeat throughout the years had me very cautious about rebranding myself and putting my focus back on building my business. It was something that was nagging at my soul that I had to keep moving in that direction. I had to recover and rise above every setback in my journey as a business owner. I never thought I could say this before because I thought things had to be perfect, but I am blessed, happy and highly favored.

Today, I am so humbled to God who has allowed me to be in the position in my life right now. I am re-married; we have a blended family of five strong African American men ranging from (12-28). My husband and I serve in our ministry as an Elder-Elect and Minister; we own nine rental properties, a Holistic Healing Center, a Home Health Care Agency, Partners in a Car Dealership, Credit Restoration Business, Foreign Currency Exchange Business, a Life Insurance Business and a Real Estate Company.

When I've tried to do things in my own strength and timing, at the end of the day, it failed. I had to repent, turn away from myself and all my negativity to get back into God's flow, which is Matthew 6:33, "Seek ye' first the Kingdom of God and all of His righteous and all these things shall be added unto you." Here is the formula that I learned from my Apostle Clarence Langston: *in order to build your business with a strong foundation, it must be built-- slow, straight, steady, strong so that it will be successful.*

I never thought I'd be here, sharing my journey of business ownership to the world and being transparent about me so that others can be encouraged. This is what I want to tell you: Don't give up on your dream(s). God has given you something special designed just for you. There is a message bottled up inside of you that you must share through your business, which is your ministry. People need to be inspired and what you have to share can bless someone's life. I know it can be scary taking that first step but don't be afraid. FEAR is, False Evidence Appearing Real. It comes to paralyze you from moving ahead. It tries to stop you from fulfilling your purpose. Don't let fear paralyze you, instead allow faith to make you LEAP into the ministry and business God has for you. You won't regret your decision! Stay consistent with God and Lean not unto your own understanding and in ALL your ways acknowledge Him and He will direct your path, Proverbs 3: 5-6. This may sound like a church cliché, but this is my truth and my truth has made me free. Until next time, be blessed.

Business Broker, Selina R. Wells started out her business part-time providing credit restoration in 1998, after realizing she had credit challenges of her own when seeking to purchase a home.

Through her company, Nationwide Community Development, Wells is on a mission to, "...make positive impact, one business and one person at a time. Selina R. Wells, plan is to develop these strong communities by helping them utilize credit for acquisition of real estate and create asset protection portfolio's through various financial and insurance plans."

Wells', (founded in 2020), Selina R. Wells & Associates which is parent company for the, "S.R. Wells Media Group" brand. S.R. Wells Media Group, produces workshops, training, multi-media (info) product and resources for people serious about building business' that last for generations.

CONTACT:

selinarwells@gmail.com
P.O. Box 76142
Lathrup Village, MI. 48076

OFFICE: 313-516-2004

FAX: 248-750-1540

ONLINE: Facebook (Pages)

"NWCDLLC" http://www.facebook.com/nwcdllc
"SELINARWELLS" http://www.facebook.com/selinarwells
@business_and_Real_Estate – Instagram

Chapter 10

Life After Loss

Audra Blyther

No parent should have to bury their child. Losing a child is not like losing a parent, relative or best friend. For women, in particular, the loss cannot be measured, as the pain cuts like shattered glass, tearing at your soul from the inside out. Women were designed to be the vessel by which new life is formed. Not being able to fulfill that promise can leave you feeling empty, worthless and inadequate. Broken.

Unfortunately, I can speak from experience.

My life, up until that point of losing my baby, had been filled with several devastating blows of physical and mental abuse by people who I trusted, like my family and spouse. The first time I was assaulted, I felt like it was my fault and that I needed to change I stayed in that relationship for 5years thinking I could make it better and fix it. Time after time, I found myself on the losing end of the stick, with the deck stacked against me. All my life, I had to fight and crawl my way out of the depths of hell. And just when I felt I was on somewhat solid ground, As if life hadn't thrown me enough blows already after crawling from the depths of hell and trying to heal from a lifetime of trauma, physical and mental abuse, I then experienced one of the most traumatic incidents that could happen to a woman, happened to me. I suffered a miscarriage at four months. As his little heartbeat was still beating on the monitor, I cried and begged them to save my baby but to no avail.

My cries went unanswered and my pleas fell upon deaf ears as this horrific nightmare continued to unfold. I lay there begging for an actual doctor, as the interns scrambled about the room, seemingly unsure of what to do to stop the pain and the premature birth of my unborn child. Then suddenly, my precious little stillborn baby boy was taken away, and a doctor came in to forcibly remove the afterbirth because my body had shut down. After hours of agony, all energy and strength were spent. There was little left of my mind, my sanity and my desire to live soon followed. I was an empty shell of a human being, certainly not a woman or a good mother, because if in fact I was a good mother, I would have been be nurturing and carry a healthy little baby boy inside my womb to full term.

I blamed the hospital, I blamed the doctors, the nurses, God, family, loved ones, stress and anything else that I could think of. Most of all, I blamed myself. I didn't leave the hospital with my baby boy, but depression, anxiety, resentment, anger and suicidal thoughts were my companions.

I suffered greatly; my family suffered as well. I knew that I had to seek therapy and instead of pushing my family and friends away, I needed their love and support now more than ever. I had to let go of the anger and bitterness. I had to let go of the what-ifs, the would've, should've and could've. Now this did not happen overnight, and there were many tears and many days of screaming to the heavens, "wWhy me?". What many don't know is that I also suffered two other miscarriages, while trying to deal and heal from the first tragic lost, all within two years' time??? Give a timeline..

As time life went on, I think I grew numb and just began to go through the motions of healing. This was a daily process that required time and patience. I began to pray and reach out to start my recovery. It has been a game changer. Therapy has played a major component in my wellbeing healing and has helped me deal ing with my depression and losst.

During therapy, I met some pretty amazing women who were also dealing with trauma. It was at this time that I realized that there were so many women of us who were broken, hurting from past pain and lacking confidence in themselves. I desired to connect with and help other women heal and transform their lives through uniting and sharing their stories. It was time for us to take off our masks and stop hiding behind our pain. It was time to unveil, surrender our cares unto God and go before the throne, unabashedly and unapologetically and transform our fear into action. We came together with an anthology to help others heal as we did. "Unveiled: Unmasking the Pain" was born, containing p. Powerful, riveting truths of nine9 brave and beautiful sisters uniting their voices and sharing their personal stories of survival. Unveiling the truth of domestic violence, mental illness, childhood trauma, eating disorders, pain after experiencing a miscarriage, the death of a loved one and surviving sexual assault. We also created a Followed by the study guide, "Unveiled: Going Beyond the Pain. A Journey to Healing & Self Discovery.

Designed to help the reader learn the importance of breaking down the walls of fear and stagnation. Learn the art and the beauty of forgiveness. Your life will be transformed and your mindset renewed, as you discover who you truly are through self-reflection. You will have the tools to start creating a vision for a better tomorrow by setting achievable goals, using proper planning and time management. By sharpening these skills you will be well on your way to thriving and living a life of joy and peace on purpose.

In conclusion, know that life will throw you curveballs and trauma will happen. I learned that we all will experience trauma at some point and time in our lives. However, it is what we do with that trauma that will affect our future relationships and alter the rest of our lives. Healing and moving beyond the pain is essential.

Life will not always be sunshine and roses and we have to learn how to adapt to change, move beyond the victim stage and do the healing work in order to live victoriously and more abundantly.

Take every opportunity to learn and grow from life's experiences. Never be afraid to share your story, seek help, counseling, therapy and to build a support system. Surround yourself with those who love you and will push you to be and do better. Your happiness is your responsibility, so choose joy and focus on the positive in your life. I no longer feel unfulfilled. I have stopped the blame game and embraced the family that I have been blessed with even more. My life is in God's hand and plan. There has been purpose in my pain.

AUDRA BLYTHER has a servants heart and the passion to help others.

A loving mother, mentor & certified life coach, ordained minister, and a wedding officiant, she is also an author.

The founder of nonprofit organization DIVINE TREASURE. Creator of the beauty unleashed health & fitness movement and creator of beautiful sisters united: WOMEN EMPOWERMENT NETWORK.

Audra is dedicated to helping others. She is committed to changing the lives of those she encounter through sharing the word of god, showing love, motivating others to successfully reach their full potential and by doing selfless acts of kindness to help those in her community.